ADAM HAMILTON

FINAL
WORDS

FROM THE CROSS

Leader Guide
by Ella Robinson

Abingdon Press / Nashville

FINAL WORDS FROM THE CROSS
Leader Guide

Copyright © 2011 by Abingdon Press

All rights reserved.
Except as noted, no part of this work may be reproduced or transmitted in any form or by any means, electronic or mechanical, including photocopying and recording, or by any information storage or retrieval system, except as may be expressly permitted by the 1976 Copyright Act or in writing from the publisher. Requests for permission should be addressed in writing to Abingdon Press, 201 Eighth Avenue South, Nashville, TN 37203, or e-mail: permissions@abingdonpress.com.

This book is printed on acid-free, elemental chlorine-free paper.

All scripture quotations, unless noted otherwise, are taken from the New Revised Standard Version of the Bible, copyright 1989 by the Division of Christian Education of the National Council of the Churches of Christ in the United States of America. Used by permission. All rights reserved.

Scripture quotations marked (ESV) are from The Holy Bible, English Standard Version®, copyright © 2001 by Crossway, a publishing ministry of Good News Publishers. Used by permission. All rights reserved.

Scripture quotations marked (NIV) are taken from the Holy Bible, NEW INTERNATIONAL VERSION®, NIV®. Copyright © 1973, 1978, 1984, 2011 by Biblica, Inc.™ Used by permission of Zondervan. All rights reserved worldwide. www.zondervan.com. The "NIV" and "New International Version" are trademarks registered in the United States Patent and Trademark Office by Biblica, Inc.™

Scripture quotations noted CEB are from the Common English Bible. Copyright © 2011 by the Common English Bible. All rights reserved. Used by permission. www.CommonEnglishBible.com.

978-1-4267-4684-0

11 12 13 14 15 16 17 18 19 20 — 10 9 8 7 6 5 4 3 2 1

MANUFACTURED IN THE UNITED STATES OF AMERICA

Contents

How to Use
This Leader Guide

Final Words From the Cross is a book-and-video based small-group study that explores the seven statements that Jesus spoke from the cross and the meaning of Jesus' dying words for our lives today.

This study is designed to coincide with the six weeks of Lent. It includes a postscript, "The Words After That," as an Easter meditation on the words Jesus spoke following his resurrection, truly the final words Jesus spoke while walking this earth. The program is appropriate for adults of all ages and stages of the Christian walk. It may be used as a stand-alone study by Sunday school classes and other small groups, or as part of a congregational emphasis and outreach event during the season of Lent.

Whether you will be leading a stand-alone study or joining other small groups in a congregational emphasis and outreach event, you should emphasize the importance of Adam Hamilton's *Final Words From the Cross,* the book that anchors the program. You'll want to encourage group members to use the corresponding chapters of the book in their preparation and follow-up for group sessions. Ideally, participants should have the opportunity to purchase copies of the book prior to your first group session. If this is not possible, introduce them to the book during your first group session and try to obtain copies prior to your second session.

A Quick Overview

As group leader, your role will be to facilitate the weekly sessions using this leader guide and the accompanying video/DVD. Because no two groups are alike, this guide has been designed to give you flexibility and choice in tailoring the sessions for your group. You may choose one of the following format options, or adapt these as you wish to meet the schedule and needs of your particular group. (Note: The times indicated within parentheses are merely estimates. You may move at a faster or slower pace, making adjustments as necessary to fit your schedule.)

Basic Option: 60 minutes

Opening Prayer	(2 minutes)
Biblical Foundation	(3 minutes)
Video Presentation	(15 minutes)
Group Discussion	(30 minutes)
Taking It Home	(5 minutes)
Closing Prayer	(< 5 minutes)

Extended Option: 90 minutes

Opening Prayer	(2 minutes)
Biblical Foundation	(3 minutes)
Opening Activity	(10-15 minutes)
Video Presentation	(15 minutes)
Group Discussion	(30 minutes)
Group Activity	(15 minutes)
Taking It Home	(5 minutes)
Closing Prayer	(< 5 minutes)

Although you are encouraged to adapt the sessions to meet your needs, you also are encouraged to make prayer and

Scripture reading regular components of the weekly group sessions. Feel free to use the opening and closing prayers provided here, the prayer/invitation at the end of each chapter of *Final Words From the Cross,* or create your own prayers. Whichever option you select, the intent is to "cover" the group session in prayer, acknowledging that only because of God's mercy and grace have we been forgiven of our sins. Scripture verses provided for each session are intended to serve as a biblical foundation for the group session as well as for participants' continuing reflection during the following week.

In addition to the components outlined above, the following "leader helps" are provided for each group session:

Key Insight   (summary of main points)

Leader Extra   (helpful information summarized)

Notable Quote   (noteworthy quote from the program)

You may use these helps for your personal preparation only, or you may choose to incorporate them into the group session in some way. For example, you might choose to review the Key Insights from the video either before or after group discussion, incorporate the Leader Highlights into group discussion, or close with the Notable Quote.

At the end of the materials provided for each group session, you will find a reproducible participant handout. This handout includes the Key Insights from the video and "Taking It Home" application exercises for the coming week. Each week you'll want to remind participants that these exercises will help them get the most out of this study. The participants are the ones who determine whether this will be just another group study or a transformational experience that will have a lasting and positive impact on their lives.

Helpful Hints

Here are a few helpful hints for preparing and leading the weekly group sessions.

- Become familiar with the material before the group session. If possible, watch the video/DVD segment in advance.
- Photocopy the participant handout before the group session, making as many copies as you will need for your group.
- Choose the various components you will use during the group session, including the specific discussion questions you plan to cover. (Highlight these or put a checkmark beside them.) Remember, you do not have to use all the questions provided, and you even can create your own.
- Secure a TV and video/DVD player in advance; oversee room setup.
- Begin and end on time.
- Be enthusiastic. Remember, you set the tone for the class.

If you are a first-time leader, remember that many characters in the Bible were hesitant and unsure of accepting God's call to lead, but God never abandoned any of them. Rest assured that God will be with you, too. After all, Jesus promised, "I am with you always, to the end of the age" (Matthew 28:20).

Session 1
"Father, Forgive Them..."

Getting Started

Session Goals

This session is intended to help participants...

- better grasp the importance of Jesus' final words.
- understand that Jesus, the Lamb of God, bore the weight of all humanity's sin so that we would be forgiven.
- realize that God's mercy and grace are gifts.
- understand how to make the most of the study through personal reflection and growing closer to God.

Opening Prayer

Dear God, our merciful Father, thank you for forgiving us when we did not know what we were doing. Even as we remained sinners, you sacrificed your only son to suffer and die for us. You have shown us mercy and given us grace. As we begin this study of your son's final words, open our ears, our hearts, and our minds so that we might learn more about you and your eternal love for us. Father, we praise your name. Amen.

Biblical Foundation

As they led him away, they seized a man, Simon of Cyrene, who was coming from the country, and they laid the cross on

*him, and made him carry it behind Jesus....When they came
to the place that is called The Skull, they crucified Jesus there
with the criminals, one on his right and one on his left. Then
Jesus said, "Father, forgive them; for they do not know what
they are doing." (Luke 23:26, 33-34a)*

Opening Activity

Create a list of people who watched as Jesus was crucified. Have participants call out people as you write them on a
board or chart. Do not discuss this list now but refer back to it
at the end of this session, at which time you should add the
names of each group participant.

Learning Together

Video Presentation

Play the video/DVD segment for Session 1.
Running Time: 10:09

Key Insights

1. It is not surprising that the first words spoken by Jesus from
   the cross were a prayer.
2. Our need for forgiveness and God's willingness to give it
   are two of the major themes of the Bible.
3. The central focus of the gospel is grace and God's mercy—
   not sin.
4. On the cross, the sins of the world—all the hatred, unfaithfulness, bigotry, poverty, violence, and death—were placed
   upon the "Lamb of God, who takes away the sins of the
   world" (John 1:29 NIV).

Leader Highlights

- Read about Passover in Exodus 12. After the Israelites were freed from slavery, God instructed them to observe three annual festivals; the first was called the Feast of Unleavened Bread or Passover (Exodus 23:15). During this festival the Israelites showed their thankfulness to God for delivering them from slavery.
- God commanded Moses to atone for the people's sins every year by bringing two goats before the Lord. One would be slaughtered, the other sent away into the wilderness (see Leviticus 16).
- Paul compared Jesus to the Passover lamb (1 Corinthians 5:7).

Group Discussion

1. Why do you think the Roman soldiers chose the season of Passover to crucify Jesus? Refer participants to Leviticus 16 and lead them to explore the meaning of the word *scapegoat.*
2. Discuss the act of crucifixion (see information in *Final Words From the Cross,* Chapter 1). Explain why speaking would be painful and require great effort from a person being crucified.
3. List three reasons why Jesus' statements from the cross are especially significant.
4. Whom did Jesus pray for when he said, "Father, forgive them; for they do not know what they are doing"?

Group Activity

- Play a recording of the African-American spiritual, "Were You There?" (A free download of the hymn is available at http://patriot.net/-bmcgin/christmusic.html.)
- Call attention to the list of people that were in attendance at

Jesus' crucifixion that the group made at the beginning of this session. At this time add the name of each participant, including yourself, to the list.

• Divide participants into two or more groups and give each group a copy of the words to the hymn. Ask each group to write an account of Jesus' crucifixion from the point of view of a person in the crowd other than Simon of Cyrene. When you come back together, briefly compare and discuss the accounts.

Wrapping Up

Taking It Home

Explain that this leader guide provides two resources in each session plan to help participants consider and apply what they have learned.

First, of course, is Adam Hamilton's book *Final Words From the Cross.* Encourage participants to read each chapter in advance of the group session and then bring their copy of the book to the session. If they have not yet read Chapter 1, encourage them to do so this week.

Second is the participant handout (see last page of this session). Pass out copies, making sure to review the "Taking It Home" application exercises included on the handout. Encourage participants to complete the activities during the coming week. *The handout may be photocopied for group use.*

Notable Quote

"On the cross Jesus' first words demonstrate God's willingness to forgive our sins, and they call us to become people who follow in his path—people who can pray, 'Father, forgive them; for they do not know what they are doing.'" (*Final Words From the Cross,* Chapter 1)

Closing Prayer

Lord God, thank you for this time of learning and sharing. We're grateful for your Word and the ability to read and study about you and your mercy. Help us to consider the insights we've gained today and use them as we learn to forgive others as you have forgiven us. As we continue our study in the weeks ahead, enable us to understand more fully your plan for our lives and help us to follow in your path. Amen.

Participant Handout

Session 1
"Father, Forgive Them..."

As they led him away, they seized a man, Simon of Cyrene, who was coming from the country, and they laid the cross on him, and made him carry it behind Jesus.... When they came to the place that is called The Skull, they crucified Jesus there with the criminals, one on his right and one on his left. Then Jesus said, "Father, forgive them; for they do not know what they are doing." (Luke 23:26, 33-34a)

Key Insights
1. It is not surprising that the first words spoken by Jesus from the cross were a prayer.
2. Our need for forgiveness and God's willingness to give it are two of the major themes of the Bible.
3. The central focus of the gospel is grace and God's mercy—not sin.
4. On the cross, the sins of the world—all the hatred, unfaithfulness, bigotry, poverty, violence, and death—were placed upon the "Lamb of God, who takes away the sins of the world" (John 1:29 NIV).

Taking It Home
- Jesus spent much of his ministry teaching about the importance of forgiving others. Beginning with the Sermon on the Mount (Matthew 5:7), search your Bible to find examples of Jesus' teaching about forgiveness.
- Are you dealing with feelings of hurt or resentment because of another person's actions? What steps could you take to follow in Jesus' path and to be able to pray, "Father, forgive them; for they do not know what they are doing"?

Session 2
"Today You Will Be With Me in Paradise"

Getting Started

Session Goals
This session is intended to help participants...

- realize that salvation is a gift from God.
- note that Jesus associated with sinners, modeling God's great mercy and grace.
- understand that we are to love the people Jesus loved.
- reflect on the fact that God, forgiving a criminal, will also forgive us.
- understand that through his suffering, death, and resurrection, Jesus was ensuring our eternal destiny, removing the curse that had banished humankind from Paradise.

Opening Prayer
Dear God, we have come together today in search of knowledge about you and your son Jesus. Clear from our thoughts all hindrances, and allow us to focus on you and your Word. Help us to become better at associating with all people whom you put along our paths. Give us courage to dine with sinners even when our friends do not understand. Amen.

Biblical Foundation

Two others also, who were criminals, were led away to be put to death with him. . . . One of the criminals who were hanged there kept deriding him and saying, "Are you not the Messiah? Save yourself and us!" But the other rebuked him, saying, "Do you not fear God, since you are under the same sentence of condemnation? And we indeed have been condemned justly, for we are getting what we deserve for our deeds, but this man has done nothing wrong." Then he said, "Jesus, remember me when you come into your kingdom." He replied, "Truly I tell you, today you will be with me in Paradise." (Luke 23:32, 39-43)

Opening Activity

Ask participants to work individually. Provide several magazines that have photos of landscapes, seascapes, animals, plants, and other magazines that have photos of luxurious items—diamonds, elaborate furniture, and so forth. Provide scissors, glue, and a half-sheet of poster board for each participant. Ask them to make a collage of what they envision Paradise to be. Encourage participants to share their collage and their thoughts regarding Paradise.

Lead participants in a discussion of the references to gardens in the Gospel stories of Jesus' final days. Include Jesus' prayer in the garden of Gethsemane, his burial in a garden tomb, and his appearance to Mary Magdalene as a gardener. Refer to Chapter 2 of the book *Final Words From the Cross* to describe a king's garden.

Learning Together

Video Presentation

Play the video/DVD segment for Session 2.
Running Time: 8:47

Key Insights
1. Even as Jesus suffered on the cross, he offered salvation to a criminal.
2. Unlike the priests and scribes, Jesus associated with sinners.
3. Through his suffering, death, and resurrection, Jesus removed the curse that had banished humankind from Paradise so that we might return to Paradise with him.

Leader Highlights
- The Greek word for *paradise* in this verse refers to the king's garden. The king's garden was a place of profound beauty. Sometimes it included a menagerie—like a zoo—combined with beautiful gardens, trees, and water features.
- When someone was honored in ancient Persia, they were given the privilege of enjoying the king's garden.
- The word *paradise* came to be used for the garden of Eden—the original King's Garden. When Adam and Eve were expelled from the garden because they disobeyed God, human beings were forbidden from ever entering that garden again. Through Jesus' suffering, death, and resurrection, he removed that curse and invited us to return to Paradise.

Group Discussion
1. Why do you think Jesus associated with sinners when the priests and scribes did not?
2. What turned the thief into a believer? Would the crowd's taunts have supplied him with the information he needed to be saved?
3. Based on Jesus' words "Today you will be with me in Paradise," what can we infer about what happens to us when we die?
4. What groups today do you think might be the equivalent of the sinners and tax collectors to whom Jesus ministered?

How would your family and friends react if you were to begin a ministry to one of those groups? Would their reaction be different if you were to begin a ministry to hospital patients? How would you respond to their reactions?

5. Do people who don't know Christ feel comfortable in your church? What can you do personally to welcome non-religious and nominally religious people?

Group Activity

Divide participants into two or more groups, and give each group a different section of a newspaper or news magazine. Ask participants to work together in their group to find examples of people in the news acting as Good Samaritans. When you come back together, briefly compare and discuss the examples.

Wrapping Up

Taking It Home

Pass out copies of the participant handout to group members, then briefly review the "Taking It Home" exercises included on the handout. Encourage participants to complete the activities during the coming week. *The handout may be photocopied for group use.*

Invite participants to read Chapter 2 of *Final Words From the Cross* this week as a follow-up to this group session. (Those reading the book in advance of group sessions will read Chapter 3 this week.)

Notable Quote

"What would happen if every one of us who professes to be a Christian would reach out to those who are lost and show them love and compassion in Jesus' name? How would the world change?" (*Final Words From the Cross*, Chapter 2)

Closing Prayer

O God, you are our God. As we participate in this study of the last words of your precious son, we see your strength and your glory. Teach us to love as Jesus loved. Teach us to reach out to others so that they might see your love through us. In Jesus' name we pray. Amen.

Participant Handout

Session 2
"Today You Will Be With Me in Paradise"

Two others also, who were criminals, were led away to be put to death with him.... One of the criminals who were hanged there kept deriding him and saying, "Are you not the Messiah? Save yourself and us!" But the other rebuked him, saying, "Do you not fear God, since you are under the same sentence of condemnation? And we indeed have been condemned justly, for we are getting what we deserve for our deeds, but this man has done nothing wrong." Then he said, "Jesus, remember me when you come into your kingdom." He replied, "Truly I tell you, today you will be with me in Paradise." (Luke 23:32, 39-43)

Key Insights
1. Even as Jesus suffered on the cross, he offered salvation to a criminal.
2. Unlike the priests and scribes, Jesus associated with sinners.
3. Through his suffering, death, and resurrection, Jesus removed the curse that had banished humankind from Paradise so that we might return to Paradise with him.

Taking It Home
- Even while Jesus was suffering a brutal death, he offered salvation to the criminal. How do you react to others when you are in a hurry, tired, or stressed?
- Do you show kindness and compassion to people whom others might ignore? How do you explain your actions to your friends?
- How can you help people who do not know Jesus Christ feel comfortable around you? Why is it important for you to know non-Christians?

Session 3
"Behold Your Son...Behold Your Mother"

Getting Started

Session Goals
This session is intended to help participants...

- understand that women were an important part of Jesus' life and ministry.
- recognize the courage of the women who witnessed Jesus' crucifixion.
- recognize Mary's role in the salvation of the human race.
- understand Jesus' love for his own mother and his command for us to care for our parents.
- identify what it means to be members of a church caring for each other.
- realize that Mary carried on Jesus' mission after he was gone.

Opening Prayer
Heavenly Father, our spirit rejoices in you. You have done great things for us. Holy is your name. Lift us up and fill us with good things. Prepare our hearts and minds as we study about Jesus and his last words to Mary and to John. Guide us in the ways we are to apply his words. In Jesus' name. Amen.

Biblical Foundation

Now there stood by the cross of Jesus His mother, and His mother's sister, Mary the wife of Clopas, and Mary Magdalene. When Jesus therefore saw His mother, and the disciple whom He loved standing by, He said to His mother, "Woman, behold your son!" Then He said to the disciple, "Behold your mother!" And from that hour that disciple took her to his own home. (John 19:25-27 NKJV)

Opening Activity

Ask participants to search their Bibles for examples of Jesus' interaction with women. Have them search for examples of Paul's interaction with women also. As participants find the examples, write them on a board or a chart.

Then, lead a discussion of the role of women in spreading the gospel story, both in biblical times and today. Point out the important role that Mary played in the salvation of the human race and in the life of Jesus.

Learning Together

Video Presentation

Play the video/DVD segment for Session 3.
Running Time: 10:26

Key Insights

1. Throughout the history of the Christian faith, Mary has been seen as a second Eve.
2. Mary, the mother of Jesus, is the single most important human being to God's saving plans aside from Jesus.
3. John was the only disciple at Jesus' crucifixion.
4. Women played a significant role in Jesus' ministry.

5. Contrary to the cultural ways of his day, Jesus regularly showed compassion, mercy, and love toward women.
6. Even as he was dying on the cross, Jesus expressed concern for his mother. He asked John to care for her and for his mother to accept John's protection and care.

Leader Highlights

- During biblical times, women were considered inferior to men. Although they were expected to abide by the law, they were not allowed to learn to read or study. Jesus did not agree with this practice. In Luke 10:38-42, he encouraged Mary to sit at his feet and learn.
- Jesus thought of women as being equal in rank with men as daughters of Abraham (Luke 13:16).
- Paul addressed men and women equally in his letters (Philippians 4:2; Philemon 2).
- Paul recognized women as co-workers, deacons, apostles, emissaries, official delegates, prophets, and leaders of house churches (Romans 16:6, 12; 1 Corinthians 16:19; Philippians 4:3).
- In Galatians 3:28, Paul says, "There is neither Jew nor Gentile, neither slave nor free, nor is there male and female, for you are all one in Christ Jesus" (NIV).

Group Discussion

Ask a participant to read the fifth commandment aloud (Exodus 20:12). Then lead a discussion of how Jesus honored his mother when he said, "Woman, here is your son."

Group Activity

Ask participants: What is our responsibility as children and as members of the church regarding taking caring of one another? Why is this becoming more important today?

Brainstorm ways your group or church can minister to others within the church (for example, to the elderly who have no family, to parents whose children have died, and to other groups). Develop a plan of action for this type of ministry.

Wrapping Up

Taking It Home
Pass out copies of the participant handout to group members, then briefly review the "Taking It Home" exercises included on the handout. Encourage participants to complete the activities during the coming week. *The handout may be photocopied for group use.*

Invite participants to read Chapter 3 of *Final Words From the Cross* this week as a follow-up to this group session. (Those reading the book in advance of group sessions will read Chapter 4 this week.)

Notable Quote
"Mary paints a picture for us of authentic discipleship and radical faithfulness to God." (*Final Words From the Cross*, Chapter 3)

Closing Prayer
Our father in heaven, hallowed be your name. As we take your precious son's last words out into the world, shine your light before us and guide us along the path you have made for us. Lead us to honor and help our parents, and to care for others as you care for us. In Jesus' holy name we pray. Amen.

Participant Handout

Session 3
"Behold Your Son ... Behold Your Mother"

Now there stood by the cross of Jesus His mother, and His mother's sister, Mary the wife of Clopas, and Mary Magdalene. When Jesus therefore saw His mother, and the disciple whom He loved standing by, He said to His mother, "Woman, behold your son!" Then He said to the disciple, "Behold your mother!" And from that hour that disciple took her to his own home. (John 19:25-27 NKJV)

Key Insights
1. Throughout the history of the Christian faith, Mary has been seen as a second Eve.
2. Mary, the mother of Jesus, is the single most important human being to God's saving plans aside from Jesus.
3. John was the only disciple at Jesus' crucifixion.
4. Women played a significant role in Jesus' ministry.
5. Contrary to the cultural ways of his day, Jesus regularly showed compassion, mercy, and love toward women.
6. Even as he was dying on the cross, Jesus expressed concern for his mother. He asked John to care for her and for his mother to accept John's protection and care.

Taking It Home
• Look in the Gospels for information about Mary, the mother of Jesus. Include Luke 1:46-55; Matthew 27:55-61; 28:1-10; and John 19:25-27. Using the information you find, create a timeline of Mary's life.
• Why have people throughout history thought of Mary as the second Eve?
• How can you honor your parents? How can you care for the elderly in your church who have no family? How can you minister to parents whose children have died?

Session 4
"My God, My God, Why Have You Forsaken Me?"

Getting Started

Session Goals

This session is intended to help participants...

- recognize the dangers of mob mentality.
- understand that because Jesus experienced human emotions he can understand how we feel.
- explore the meaning of sacrificial love.

Opening Prayer

Heavenly Father, we praise your name. Let your light shine bright for us as we study the final words of your son. Make us aware of the effects of bullying, taunting and violence. Guide us away from these hurtful actions and toward those who are hurting. Give us the confidence to stand up, reach out, and defend those who are the subjects of mob mentality. Amen.

Biblical Foundation

When it was noon, darkness came over the whole land until three in the afternoon. At three o'clock Jesus cried out with a loud voice, "Eloi, Eloi, lema sabachthani?" which means, "My God, my God, why have you forsaken me?" When some of the bystanders heard it, they said, "Listen, he is

*calling for Elijah."And someone ran, filled a sponge with
sour wine, put it on a stick, and gave it to him to drink.*

(Mark 15:33-36a)

Opening Activity

Ask participants to describe examples of bullying, taunting, and violence that they know of or have witnessed. Write
the examples on a chart or board, then lead a discussion of mob
mentality as described in Chapter 4 of *Final Words From the
Cross*.

Learning Together

Video Presentation

Play the video/DVD segment for Session 4.
Running Time: 9:05

Key Insights

1. Mob mentality increased the taunting and humiliation that
   Jesus experienced on the cross.
2. The people who led the charge in dehumanizing and humiliating Jesus were the most pious people in the community. Deeply committed Jews, they were the priests and
   scribes.
3. Jesus taught us to suffer and sacrifice so that others might
   be delivered.
4. When Jesus felt abandoned and forsaken by God, he chose
   to pray and worship.

Leader Highlights

• Germans murdered millions of Jews; the Soviets murdered
  millions of their own people; the Khmer Rouge murdered

millions of Cambodians; Hutu of Rwanda took machetes to 800,000 of their fellow church members, co-workers, and neighbors who were Tutsi. Many of the people involved in these unforgettable atrocities claimed to be Christians.

- The words "My God, my God, why have you forsaken me?" are the first stanza of a hymn that most of the Jews in Jesus' day would have known: Psalm 22. The hymn describes a time when David was suffering at the hands of his enemies. Events described in this hymn can be seen as parallel with what happened at the cross.

Group Discussion

1. How do you think it was possible for devout, pious people who were celebrating the Passover, hoping and praying for the coming of the Messiah, to become a taunting crowd at Jesus' crucifixion?
2. What did Jesus do when he felt forsaken by God? What do you do when you experience tough times?
3. Explain the meaning of the term *sacrificial love*. Name some examples of people in your community exhibiting sacrificial love.
4. Discuss situations in which Christians today sacrifice to show God's love toward other human beings.
5. What kinds of things cause you to say hurtful words about others or to act in un-Christian ways?
6. How do you feel when you are told that you cannot have something that you want? How do you think Jesus felt? What did he do?

Group Activity

Ask participants to turn to Psalm 22 and compare David's account of suffering with Jesus' suffering on the cross.

Wrapping Up

Taking It Home

Pass out copies of the participant handout to group members, then briefly review the "Taking It Home" exercises included on the handout. Encourage participants to complete the activities during the coming week. *The handout may be photocopied for group use.*

Invite participants to read Chapter 4 of *Final Words From the Cross* this week as a follow-up to this group session. (Those reading the book in advance of group sessions will read Chapter 5 this week.)

Notable Quote

"The gospel calls us to a life in which we risk, sacrifice, and give ourselves so that others might know the love of God." (*Final Words From the Cross,* Chapter 4)

Closing Prayer

Dear God, darkness overwhelms us. We hear people taunted and bullied. Rage and hatred are common. Violence swarms all around us. Keep us from the temptation to join the crowd and humiliate others. Help us to be willing to sacrifice so that others might be delivered. Amen.

Participant Handout

Session 4
"My God, My God, Why Have You Forsaken Me?"

When it was noon, darkness came over the whole land until three in the afternoon. At three o'clock Jesus cried out with a loud voice, "Eloi, Eloi, lema sabachthani?" which means, "My God, my God, why have you forsaken me?" When some of the bystanders heard it, they said, "Listen, he is calling for Elijah." And someone ran, filled a sponge with sour wine, put it on a stick, and gave it to him to drink.

(Mark 15:33-36a)

Key Insights
1. Mob mentality increased the taunting and humiliation that Jesus experienced on the cross.
2. The people who led the charge in dehumanizing and humiliating Jesus were the most pious people in the community. Deeply committed Jews, they were the priests and scribes.
3. Jesus taught us to suffer and sacrifice so that others might be delivered.
4. When Jesus felt abandoned and forsaken by God, he chose to pray and worship.

Taking It Home
- Think about the last time you lost your temper and reacted toward someone with rage. How did you feel during your rage? How did you feel afterward?
- Now think of the last time you risked, sacrificed, and gave of yourself so that someone might know the love of God. Has the sharing of God's love cost you anything or caused you any discomfort?

Session 5
"I Thirst"

Getting Started

Session Goals

This session is intended to help participants...

- explore John's use of metaphors in his recording of Jesus' crucifixion.
- understand that Jesus experienced human emotions, including hopelessness and helplessness.
- think about why Jesus refused to drink the wine mixed with poison.
- realize that sometimes following Jesus requires us to undergo suffering or discomfort.

Opening Prayer

Heavenly Father, we sing praise to your name. You have made us rejoice, Lord, by what you have done. We gather in your name, seeking to learn more about you and your precious son, Jesus. Guide us as we study his final words. Clear our minds and help us focus on you. Amen.

Biblical Foundation

After this, Jesus, knowing that all was now finished, said (to fulfill the Scripture), "I thirst." A jar full of sour wine stood there, so they put a sponge full of the sour wine on a hyssop branch and held it to his mouth. (John 19:28-29 ESV)

Opening Activity

Lead a discussion of how Jesus uses the metaphor of drinking water to refer to salvation. Ask participants to work together to find references to thirst and drinking water in the Gospels.

Learning Together

Video Presentation

Play the video/DVD segment for Session 5.
Running Time: 10:16

Key Insights

1. The phrase "I thirst" is another example of Jesus' humanity.
2. On multiple occasions, Jesus used the metaphor of drinking as a way of describing the suffering he would endure on the cross.
3. The phrase "I thirst" indicates that Jesus was willing to take on humanity's suffering, sin, and hatred.
4. Another interpretation of the phrase "I thirst" is that the cup was now nearly empty, and Jesus' time of suffering was drawing to a close.
5. In John 4, Jesus refers to living water. As water is essential for sustaining life, perhaps "I thirst" meant Jesus' earthly life was nearing its end.
6. Hyssop was used in Exodus 12:22 to dab the blood of a sacrificed lamb on the doorpost of Israelites' homes; in John 19:29 a sponge was attached to the hyssop branch (which would be quite small and flexible) and used to dampen

Jesus' lips. Perhaps the use of the hyssop branch at Jesus' crucifixion indicates Jesus' power to deliver us from death.

Leader Highlights

- There are three different Gospel accounts of the offer of drink to Jesus at his crucifixion.
    1. He was offered wine mixed with myrrh (Mark 15: 23) or gall (Matthew 27:34). Although scholars continue to debate the purpose of the additive, *Final Words From the Cross* offers two possible explanations. The additive could have been used to make criminals sick to the stomach, inducing vomiting and adding to the pain of crucifixion. Or, perhaps the ingredient was used as a poison to hasten death or weaken the pain.
    2. After Jesus was nailed to the cross, the people taunted him, offering sour wine as a toast that they kept just out of his reach (Luke 23:36-37).
    3. Matthew, Mark, and John record that someone near the cross used a stick with a sponge on the end to soak up sour wine and hold it to Jesus' lips (Matthew 27:48; Mark 15:36; John 19:29).
- In the Bible, wine is often associated with blessings, celebration, and happiness. It is also referred to as a judgment, punishment, and evil.
- Sour wine was cheap wine commonly drunk by the poor and by the Roman soldiers. It also was known as wine vinegar; it had a bitter taste.

Group Discussion

1. Why do you think Jesus said in Luke 2:18 that he would not drink again from the fruit of the vine until the coming of the kingdom of God?
2. Why would the women who stood at the cross offer Jesus wine with poison in it? Discuss why Jesus refused the drink.

3. Compare Jesus' thirst in John 4:1-26 with his thirst in John 19:28-29. How did these two incidents have similar results?
4. What is the significance of using a hyssop stick to lift a sponge drenched with wine up to Jesus on the cross?
5. How do you think the others in the crowd responded to the person who offered a wine-soaked sponge to Jesus? How would the Roman guards have responded to this act?

Group Activity

Divide participants into three groups. Ask one group to search their Bibles for examples of wine used for celebration. Ask another group to search their Bibles for examples of wine referred to in a negative way. And ask the third group to search their Bibles for examples of water used to quench thirst. Lead a discussion of these findings.

Wrapping Up

Taking It Home

Pass out copies of the participant handout to group members, then briefly review the "Taking It Home" exercises included on the handout. Encourage participants to complete the activities during the coming week. *The handout may be photocopied for group use.*

Invite participants to read Chapter 5 of *Final Words From the Cross* this week as a follow-up to this group session. (Those reading the book in advance of group sessions can read Chapter 6 this week.)

Notable Quote

"Jesus took the uncomfortable way, the inconvenient way, the way most of us don't want to go." (*Final Words From the Cross,* Chapter 5)

Closing Prayer

Lord God, thank you for the truths you've shown us today through this study. Thank you for extending a cup of cool water to each of us when we were thirsting. Open our eyes, our ears, and our hearts to those around us who are thirsty, and give us the wisdom and strength to offer them your Living Water. Amen.

Participant Handout

Session 5
"I Thirst"

After this, Jesus, knowing that all was now finished, said (to fulfill the Scripture), "I thirst." A jar full of sour wine stood there, so they put a sponge full of the sour wine on a hyssop branch and held it to his mouth. (John 19:28-29 ESV)

Key Insights
1. The phrase "I thirst" is an example of Jesus' humanity.
2. On multiple occasions, Jesus used the metaphor of drinking to describe the suffering he would endure on the cross.
3. The phrase "I thirst" indicates that Jesus was willing to take on humanity's suffering, sin, and hatred.
4. Another interpretation of the phrase "I thirst" is that the cup was now nearly empty, and Jesus' time of suffering was drawing to a close.
5. In John 4, Jesus refers to living water. As water is essential for sustaining life, perhaps "I thirst" meant Jesus' earthly life was nearing its end.
6. Hyssop was used in Exodus 12:22 to dab the blood of a sacrificed lamb on the doorpost of Israelites' homes; in John 19:29 a sponge was attached to the hyssop branch (which would be quite small and flexible) and used to dampen Jesus' lips. Perhaps the use of the hyssop branch at Jesus' crucifixion indicates Jesus' power to deliver us from death.

Taking It Home
• Do you know someone who is thirsting? Are you willing to risk the scorn of others to give that person a drink? Would you go out of your way to offer a cool cup of water, literally or figuratively, to a thirsting person?
• Meditate on Matthew 25:40—"When you have done it for one of the least of these brothers and sisters of mine, you have done it for me" (CEB).

Session 6
"It Is Finished"..."Into Your Hands I Commit My Spirit"

Getting Started

Session Goals

This session is intended to help participants...

- explore the use of the metaphors Jesus used to describe the meaning of his death on the cross.
- understand the mission Jesus completed on the cross.
- recognize that Jesus ended his suffering by teaching us how to live each day—not in fear but in confidence and hope.

Opening Prayer

Dear God, guide us as we study your precious son's final words on the cross. We recognize the importance of your great gift of salvation through Jesus. Open our eyes, our ears, our minds, and our hearts so that we may receive all you have to tell us about your son. Equip us to take the lessons we learn in this study into the world and proclaim that Jesus lives. Amen.

Biblical Foundation

When Jesus had received the wine, he said, "It is finished."
(John 19:30a)

The curtain of the temple was torn in two. Jesus called out with a loud voice, "Father, into your hands I commit my spirit." When he had said this, he breathed his last. The centurion, seeing what had happened, praised God and said, "Surely this was a righteous man." (Luke 23:45-47NIV)

Opening Activity

Briefly discuss the literary device called metaphor, then have participants search their Bibles for examples of metaphors. Tell the group that they will be exploring Jesus' use of metaphors to describe the meaning of his death on the cross.

Learning Together

Video Presentation

Play the video/DVD segment for Session 6.
Running Time: 10:15

Key Insights

1. In the cross we see that we are sinners in need of saving. God comes to us to save us from our sin, from ourselves, and even from death.
2. God longs to forgive us; he suffers for us; and he offers us salvation that Jesus himself paid for at a great price.
3. On the cross, Jesus made a full, perfect, and sufficient sacrifice for the sins of the world once and for all.
4. Jesus' last words were not a cry of defeat and surrender, but a declaration of victory.
5. Jesus' dying words were a prayer of absolute trust in God.

Leader Highlights
- When simple or pat answers were insufficient, the Bible writers used literary devices such as metaphors to better explain events and concepts. Metaphors compare one thing to another. In themselves, they are not the meaning; they are a way of getting at the meaning. In other words, they are a vehicle, a tool.
- The Temple, God's presence on earth, had been turned into a marketplace. When Jesus saw how the people of Jerusalem defamed God's presence, he predicted the destruction of the Temple. He said, "Destroy this temple, and in three days I will raise it up." But this temple would not be made with hands. Jesus was saying that he would stand in place of the Temple as the presence of God (John 2:13-22; Mark 13:1-2; 14:58).
- The Temple had an elaborate, thick curtain that separated the Holy of Holies from the Holy Place. Only the high priest would enter the Holy of Holies. When Jesus died, the curtain was torn in two.
- In addition to the tearing of the curtain in the Temple, several other strange events occurred when Jesus drew his final breath—the earth shook and rocks split; tombs broke open; and the bodies of righteous people who had died came to life and were seen by many people.

Group Discussion
1. Why did Jesus quote Psalm 31:5 for his final words?
2. Discuss the significance of the tearing of the Temple curtain when Jesus died.
3. Hamilton writes, "The cross is less about economics or a courtroom.... The cross is a divine drama." Explore what he means by this statement.

4. Discuss the significance of the Roman soldier saying, "Surely this man was a righteous man."
5. Why do people try to predict the end of the world? Why is such prediction unimportant to Christians?
6. How do you express your love to your family members? How is this similar to and different from the love that Jesus expressed on the cross?

Group Activity

Ask participants to search their Bibles for passages in which Jesus spoke about the meaning of his death. Write on the board or a chart the references they find and discuss each reference. Point out Jesus' use of metaphors to describe what he was seeking to accomplish in his death. Use this list of passages to help participants if they become stuck: Matthew 16:21; John 3:16-17; John 12:32; John 12:24; Luke 22:20; Matthew 26:28; Matthew 26:1-2.

Wrapping Up

Taking It Home

Pass out copies of the participant handout to group members, then briefly review the "Taking It Home" exercises included on the handout. Encourage participants to complete the activities during the coming week. *The handout may be photocopied for group use.*

Invite participants to read Chapter 6 of *Final Words From the Cross* this week as a follow-up to this group session. (Those reading the book in advance of group sessions can read Postscript: The Words After That.)

Notable Quote

"Something astounding, amazing, and awesome was finished as Jesus died on the cross—a masterpiece of love and redemption." (*Final Words From the Cross,* Chapter 6)

Closing Prayer

Lord God, thank you for sending your precious son Jesus to bear the burden of our sins and secure for us a place in paradise. Guide us as we take into the world the lessons we have learned through this study of Jesus' last words. Allow these words to shape our lives as we follow in the footsteps of our crucified King. Amen.

Participant Handout

Session 6
"It Is Finished"..."Into Your Hands I Commit My Spirit"

When Jesus had received the wine, he said, "It is finished."
(John 19:30a)

The curtain of the temple was torn in two. Jesus called out with a loud voice, "Father, into your hands I commit my spirit." When he had said this, he breathed his last. The centurion, seeing what had happened, praised God and said, "Surely this was a righteous man." (Luke 23:45-47 NIV)

Key Insights
1. In the cross we see that we are sinners in need of saving. God comes to us to save us from our sin, from ourselves, and even from death.
2. God longs to forgive us; he suffers for us; and he offers us salvation that Jesus himself paid for at a great price.
3. On the cross, Jesus made a full, perfect, and sufficient sacrifice for the sins of the world once and for all.
4. Jesus' last words were not a cry of defeat and surrender, but a proclamation of victory.
5. Jesus' dying words were a prayer of absolute trust in God.

Taking It Home
- We do not know God's plan for us, but we do know that our suffering can be used to achieve something much greater than we could ever imagine.
- Jesus' last words on the cross were a prayer quoted from Psalm 31. He ended his suffering by teaching us how to live each day—not in fear but in confidence and hope: by placing our spirit in the Father's hands.

Postscript
The Words After That

Getting Started

Session Goals
This session is intended to help participants . . .

- understand the meaning of Christ's resurrection.
- experience the emotions of Jesus' disciples after his crucifixion and upon realizing that he did not die.
- realize that Jesus walks with us daily, even in times of our greatest despair.

Opening Prayer
Dear God, we shout joyfully to you, our Lord. We enter your presence with joy and thanksgiving. Prepare our hearts that we might hear and understand the message you have for us as we study your Word. Amen.

Biblical Foundation
Now on that same day two of them were going to a village called Emmaus, about seven miles from Jerusalem, and talking with each other about all these things that had happened. While they were talking and discussing, Jesus himself came near and went with them, but their eyes were kept from recognizing him. (Luke 24:13-16)

Opening Activity

Ask participants to describe ways they celebrate Easter. List these on one side of a chart or board. Discuss how our celebrations of Easter and Christmas are alike and/or different. Discuss reasons for the similarities and differences.

Learning Together

Video Presentation

Play the video/DVD segment for the Postscript.
Running Time: 10:11

Key Insights

1. On the road to Emmaus, the stranger did not remove his disguise or announce himself as Jesus.
2. God's way is to come to us through the stranger—or sometimes a family member or friend—to offer hope and point us toward the Resurrection.
3. After the disciples welcomed the stranger, they saw Christ.
4. As we trust in Jesus, as we believe that he died and rose again, all our problems are not solved. Rather, we find peace and the strength and courage to face life with hope.

Leader Highlights

- Emmaus was about seven miles from Jerusalem and thought to be the home of Cleopas. It would have taken about two hours to walk from Jerusalem to the city of Emmaus.
- Because Cleopas and his companion were experiencing grief and loss on their way to Emmaus, "the road to Emmaus" is now used to indicate a period of grief and loss during which time a person experiences the presence of God.

Group Discussion
1. How did Thomas respond to the presence of the risen Lord (John 20:25)? Why do you think he responded that way?
2. What is the significance of the stranger breaking bread with the disciples on the road to Emmaus?
3. Discuss ways in which this study has deepened your understanding of Jesus' last days on earth.

Wrapping Up

Taking It Home
Pass out copies of the participant handout to group members, then briefly review the "Taking It Home" exercises included on the handout. Encourage participants to complete the activities during the coming week. *The handout may be photocopied for group use.*

Invite participants to read the Postscript of *Final Words From the Cross* this week as a follow-up to this group session.

Notable Quote
"Jesus' resurrection does not remove us from our present circumstances. But it does change how we see them. We face adversity, illness, and tragedy knowing that with God they will never have the final word." (*Final Words From the Cross,* Postscript)

Closing Prayer
Lord God, keep us near the cross where "the bright and morning star sheds its beams around" us.* O Lamb of God, help us walk from day to day in the shadow of the cross. Amen.

* From "Jesus, Keep Me Near the Cross," by Fanny J. Crosby (The United Methodist Hymnal, 301).

Participant Handout

Postscript
"The Words After That"

Now on that same day two of them were going to a village called Emmaus, about seven miles from Jerusalem, and talking with each other about all these things that had happened. While they were talking and discussing, Jesus himself came near and went with them, but their eyes were kept from recognizing him. (Luke 24:13-16)

Key Insights
1. On the road to Emmaus, the stranger did not remove his disguise or announce himself as Jesus.
2. God's way is to come to us through the stranger—or sometimes a family member or friend—to offer hope and point us toward the Resurrection.
3. After the disciples welcomed the stranger, they saw Christ.
4. As we trust in Jesus, as we believe that he died and rose again, we do not find riches; all our problems are not solved. Rather, we find peace and the strength and courage to face life with hope.

Taking It Home
- Write about a time when you traveled the road to Emmaus. Explore the reason for your sorrow and tell whether and how you met Jesus along the road.
- Read Luke 24:13-52 and then write the events of Emmaus from the viewpoint of one of the disciples.